The Inspiration YOU need to Break Free!
DIVINE ORDER....
Your steps are ordered...
destiny you found this book or it found you...
Save Yourself!
When this thought entered my mind May 16, 2019, I knew
that I would dedicate my life to writing

"Self -Therapy" Books because...
"YOU have to Save Yourself before
YOU can save anyone else"
Your Future is calling for KNOWLEDGE and possible
CHANGE and you have answered the call by picking up
this book of inspiration.

I Affirm

YOU ARE AN AWESOME CHILD OF GOD

MICHELLE WHITBY
Aspiring Author of "Self-Therapy" Books
I aspire to write books to first help me then to help you!

3G Publishing, Inc.
Loganville, Ga 30052
www.3gpublishinginc.com
Phone: 1-888-442-9637

First published by 3G Publishing, Inc. August, 2020.

ISBN: 9781941247785

Printed in the United States of America

Contents

Forward

YOUR DIVINE CALL / KNOWLEDGE

A people in need of healing is what my spirit speaks to me. My dedication to answer the call. I believe God talks to us ALL in some way, in some shape or form, my thing is what takes us soooooo long to answer the call? I really admire those that get it sooner more so than later, they know their life's purpose early on. I'm definitely in the later crowd, at times I'm resentful, but truth of the matter is maybe I would not have been smart enough or wise enough to use the gifts that GOD has placed in me to use now. Maybe, just maybe my life is rolling out day by day, the way it is supposed to. Maybe this is the same for you? Before now maybe you had no reason to know or use the knowledge that you will obtain from this book. I believe that each and every day we are blessed to open our eyes and ears the Divine is whispering and constantly trying to get our attention and lead us in the right direction. Let me speak for myself, at least this has been the case for me. I say often LORD what took me soooooo long! Gods perfect timing is all I can sum it up to be and maybe before now the year 2019 I was not ready to receive his DIVINE WORD. I have a DIVINE WORD for you, "if you are fortunate enough to be born in the USA then it is not Gods intention for YOU to REMAIN in POVERTY"!

This is a story of inspiration, I promise and I hope that it is received that way, yet I know it will be received or taken as otherwise by some. I can hear the naysayers saying "who does she think she is"? I can tell you who I think I am, 1st I am an awesome child of God, I believe in the GREAT I am and that I was created to do GREAT things. This revelation is not only for me but it is also for YOU. You were born to do the GREAT things God has planted within YOU!

Life is a series of journeys, and it always starts as a whisper....

Journey defined by Dictionary.com

1. A traveling from one place to another, usually taking a rather long time; trip
2. Passage or progress from one stage to another

A series of learned experiences and journeys is definitely what led to the writing of this book.

What a journey my life has been with its twist, turns and the unforeseen. Never in a ka'zillion years could I have foreseen being led to write this book and what I have coined "The Plantation of Minimum Wage" that perpetuates PLANTATION NATION. I truly believe I was DIVINELY lead on this journey and for once I not only listened to the whispers, but in obedience I began writing as it is to encourage YOU along your life's journeys as you are called to do what you were born to do.

The Journey begins....

PLANTATION a word I had never seen plastered before my eyes until my arrival south to Georgia in 2006. Before then this word was not on my radar EVER! Being from the North it was actually quite shocking to see such a word plastered as a street name and housing subdivisions in which people actually live.

Truly perplexed because one of my immediate thoughts was why would someone want to live on the "plantation"? Well not literally but figuratively. My brain waves could not wrap my head around who would drive into a place with this name and call it home? This thought just would not leave my brain waves alone. Steady in my head.... I could not live or drive into a place that is supposed to be my retreat, my home, my residence, my sanctuary from the craziness of the world. I could not deliberately put into my psyche on a daily the word "plantation". All the negative associated with the word alone prevents me. Still thinking.... I said to myself don't they know what happened on plantations? Have they truly forgotten It was the system that kept a people in order, it was a system were people worked for pennies or nothing at all. It was a system designed to keep people at the bottom of the economic totem pole. It was a place where people barely survived, could not thrive and where many died at the hand of the slave master. I could only conclude for myself there is no way I could live on the "plantation"!

So as life would have it the journey moves on, I accepted that it is what it is, this is the norm, I guess? I reminded myself, after all I do now reside in the south. And no one else seems to be bothered by this but me, so I summed it up its just me being overly sensitive. I don't know why I have such a strong repulsion toward this word but trust and believe I will NEVER live in a housing community or subdivision titled "PLANTATION" anything!

DIVINE ENLIGHTENMENT
The Awakening....

The Journey Continues....

It starts with a thought – it is actually God speaking to YOU! Move forward is what we must do if we do not want to get stuck in "yuck". A yucky, sucky life that is. My move forward after experiencing the devasting emotions of divorce was to make my way even further south to the "Sunshine" state of Florida. I can remember so vividly.... as I was getting to know my new surroundings it was a clear picture perfect blue sky day and I was simply taking it all in and basking in the beauty before my eyes. I was all glittery like a child from the glitz of the beautiful homes and luxurious landscaping. I was just thankful for my eyes being able to see such beauty. I truly was bopping along singing my songs and enjoying the Florida sunshine when suddenly the feelings of grateful euphoria came to a screeching halt because what did my eyes suddenly see, that word plastered on so many communities!

Again, I personally truly sit in my thoughts perplexed that this name is proudly displayed. As I often have to do, I have a talk with myself to calm down, don't react – overreact, STOP being super sensitive! Myself talks continues, I don't know why I have this strong feeling about this word when no one else does? My thoughts of glee start to take a turn towards negative as my thoughts about those who reside in these big beautiful communities fester. Questions, questions, questions run through my head, is slavery really dead? Too afraid to venture into these communities I pass by bewildered , perplexed saying "what the heck"! As usual it's just me reacting to something passionately, I have these conversations with myself in search of 1st helping myself then everybody else. The activist in me has no clue as to where these thoughts of repulsion lead. I don't trust people who live in these communities! I immediately become concerned about my safety. Lord forbid I speed through or have an encounter with a resident in this hood. I fear getting stopped by the police for fear of how they will treat me. After all, their number 1 goal is to patrol the 'plantation" and maintain control. I don't think they will have any sympathy for me, I'm not of the white skinned race so they don't associate or connect with me. This racism thing is big and scary so I pass by these communities as cautious as ever.

My steps being ordered I truly cannot see exactly where this journey is/was leading me. But it was evident the day I arrived at the corporate site because I couldn't believe what was before my eyes. Although planted many years ago I now know why the seed of awareness danced in my head. Slowly but surely this situation was starting to unfold. No longer just the word of repulsion but actuality I ended up on a real life plantation without full explanation. I simply listen to this whispers inside my head. I just have to trust and believe where the DIVINE is leading me. Talking to myself and the Divine as I often do I say "Lord you've got jokes" , the Divine's rebuttal "so do you"! The Divines voice would not leave me alone it kept speaking and bothering me. I was for sure hesitant to answer this call but the prompting, again, would not leave me alone. My prayers, my questions "Lord how can little ole me take on something of this enormity"?

My first day of work I literally jerked because I realized it is the Corporate Plantation which rules this nation. Here racism reigns supreme because the white skinned people own everything! It is to them who most of us look to for work that allows us to feed our families. This system simply bothers me and I wonder why we don't do anything but simply stay the course and remain "good negros". My seeing and being in this system I wrestle with what I thought I was being lead to write which was an inspirational story. I say "Lord how can such a thing be in the 21 century of US history"? How is it I end up here being paid a wage that for sure will keep me enslaved? As life happens, as it unfolds sometimes you just cannot see where it is going or where you are being lead, this is for sure my story. I don't know why God designed it this way. I guess there is no other way to have a faith story. I'm living proof of why we just must trust and have faith. Especially when you are lead to write on the plague of racism that affects our great nation. Again, one last time I ask because doubt for sure creeps in my head…. "Lord how can little bitty ole me tackle the enormity of this BIG scary racism thing"? His response you just have to trust and believe. So I continue to move forward and to God be the glory, I accepted my assignment and got busy writing. I trust and believe the voice speaking to me and led me to write this book of inspiration that will undoubtedly continue to wake up this nation.

So child of GOD…listen to the whispers the DIVINE speaks to your mind.

The Great I AM Gifts us ALL and YOU child of God are being called to YOUR DIVINE ASSIGNMENT.....to use your gifts to first heal yourself so that you can help and heal someone else. This book of inspiration is for YOU!

This Book is Dedicated to:

Future Generations, Inspiration Rangers, Dreamers, Entrepreneurs, Small Business Owners, Parents, Corporate Companies, ALL World Changers.

To Future Generations

Young people I don't want you to get stuck on the Plantation! This book is first dedicated to you! Your parents, grandparents, aunts, uncles, cousins, have done their best to encourage and educate YOU! Just know that they cannot encourage or educate YOU pass what they don't know. I wrote this book to encourage you NOT to settle for the crap the world spits at you. You are gifted and were born for a specific purpose. I hope you take this as a book of inspiration.

To the Inspiration Rangers

It is up to you to inspire others and continue what has been started, the torch I pass to you. You are the change agents of the future. You Inspiration Ranger are to Inspire higher and encourage those around you out of this systematic generational poverty.

To the Dreamers. Entrepreneurs, or Small Business Owners….

Who are in their start up stage in which…we know startups crawl or walk before they have the capability to "RUN"…efficiently on their own. But once you are RUNNING on your own it is the expectation that you too will join the movement and be instrumental in the social change necessary to release the chains of generational poverty that keeps people enslaved.

To Parents of School Age Children

Teach your children to be GREAT NOW! And in their GREATNESS remember others so they don't leave behind another generation lost to others.

To Corporate Companies / CEO's CFO's COO's

Who make hundreds of millions even billions of dollars annually. You have the "true capability" and "authority" to stop this generational poverty. You most of all can implement the change necessary to release the chains that keep people economically enslaved.

TO ALL WORLD CHANGERS IT IS OUR DUTY TO INSTITUTE THE CHANGE NECESSARY TO MAKE OUR WORLD A BETTER PLACE.

May we ALL start and spark the discussions of the change necessary to help move a people forward and stop the blood line of perpetual poverty.

Preface

Many preachers say "a setback is a set up for a comeback", a cliché at times that is hard for many to believe. Setbacks or in other words storms we all can relate to because either we have experienced them ourselves or we know someone who has. Storms are as natural to our existence as the air we breathe, yet they are often disguised as "setbacks" because of the internal and external trauma they can cause. These storms with their apparent outwardly destruction can cause minor or life altering damage that shatters one's life and existence into many pieces. Depending on the magnitude of the storm we have to make adjustments if we are going to survive. In many instances we have no option but to clean up the mess. What I've learned is after the storm the choice is to collect what's of value use it as motivation to rebuild or the alternative remain with the broken pieces stuck in muck that can keep you dazed, confused and not knowing which way to go!

At times I relate more to the latter, dazed, confused, not knowing which way to go. I too have had difficulty believing what I have heard many preachers say "setbacks are set ups for the comeback". I have survived many storms, but the most tumultuous yet has been my divorce after 18 years of marriage it left me doubtless about a prospering future, in my mind at the time this storm was the ultimate setback! Talking about a storm that will break one into many pieces, I was no doubt shattered, dazed, confused and did not know which way to go! Initially

I was truly stuck in muck! After I realized that I had to keep living, killing myself was not an option! I picked up what was of value from this storm, moved to sunny Florida because frankly I needed to rebuild and start fresh!

Setback for the Comeback

Now back to the appearance of a what LOOKS like a "setback" because after the storm we SEE so many broken pieces all around us, it is difficult to believe it is a "SETUP for the COMEBACK". We tend to look outwardly at what we SEE and not inwardly to what we are truly called to be. I have learned that this is when my true capabilities are revealed to me.

Each storm has given me opportunity to really hear the Divines voice first out of desperation, many prayers go up during this traumatic time "Lord help me to survive this, I don't think I'm going to make it" and secondly to overcome the depression in my mind, again prayers up, "Lord this life sucks", "I'm depressed, again, I'm not going to make it". It is the during the calm after the storm that I have had to find my strength, to survive. I have no choice but to listen to the Divine guide, because of my own strength, I don't think I would make it, quitting seems like a better option. Thank God for continually speaking to me especially when I didn't want to hear there are opportunities after the storm!

Initially my negative mindset was full of doubt, doubt, and more doubt… just when I would tell my mind more negatives "I'm tired" or I would say to myself "I cannot go on another day" something good would happen, epiphanies just kept coming to me. I now think differently about storms and wholeheartedly believe that the storm is Gods way of ultimately leading us to our Destiny by giving us yet another opportunity to start fresh. I believe he strengthens us to do away with the mess so that he can lead us step by step for a specific purpose.

Emotionally and Financially after being in a relationship for 18 years, sure in my mind I was "setback", but because I sincerely believe in our Lord and Savior Jesus Christ and his biblical word, "your steps are ordered" Psalms 37:23, "I know the plans I have for you" Jeremiah 29:11. If I believe he is who he says he is then I must have faith and believe his word that "all things work out for the good of those that love God" Romans 8:28. I believe Gods promises which is his promise of a "the abundant life" John 10:10 in spite of it all. Ultimately, what you think and how you think determines your outcome after the storm. It is easy to get stuck in muck. I choose to think on and believe Gods promises. My new reality, storms give us opportunities to re-set, start fresh, and build new intentional lives!

I believe my steps have been ordered to write this book on the "Plantation on Minimum Wage" in other words PLANTATION NATION. It was not in my thoughts or plan to write such a book. I've often heard the preachers say "our thoughts are not his thoughts" Isaiah 55:8 in other words "our plans are not Gods plan". This I know for sure!

I believe It was no accident that I being the smart educated middle aged woman that I am as I pen this that I ended up on a job making barely minimum wage after I had been at the top of the middle class pay scale. The pay alone encouraged me out of my comfort zone. It was very uncomfortable for me to be working at a level beneath my true capabilities but because of my faith I took this as insight as to what I am to learn as I move on. I had to SEE for myself the predicament of those I desire to help.

If it were not for this experience, I would have remained at the top of the pay scale delusional like others and out of range of those who lives I desired to touch, those like me born into generational poverty. My eyes could see this situation was not just about me.

I'm learning it all comes together in time, during the storm we may have many questions and ask, "why me Lord", why, why, why?

Bottom line, one of the biggest storms I had to endure was a divorce. Again, I'd prayed often and asked many questions. My initial plea was "Lord please rescue me"! This life event I know firsthand leaves one dismal and confused. It was for me at the time, what appeared to be one of the biggest setbacks of my life. I was set back emotionally and financially so I thought. I had no choice but to trust and believe the voice inside leading me.

A new story begins...

Again our / my steps being ordered, here is my story of how I was "setup" to write a book I had no idea was even in me. A new destiny leading me.

I don't remember the exact year, but I think it was around "2006" when the word "Plantation" caught my eye plastered as the name of many public places in the south. My eyes could not believe what they would see and in my circle of friends it's as if these words only bothered me.

The years ticked on all the way to year "2019" the year my marriage ended. After this storm I had to practice what I preach to others. I had to take my own advice and look for the valuable pieces so that I could rebuild, restart and move on". During this time I had many conversations with myself "Michelle don't stay stuck in the muck that can keep you dazed and confused". You are still living and you've got work to do!

Because of my love for the sun and beach I continued to listen to the voice leading me to a place I have always wanted to be, sunny Florida. I had no idea that writing about the "Plantation" was part of my sunny Florida destination.

I arrived to my new sunny destination May of 2019 and as I was riding around getting to know my new sunny surroundings I could not believe what my eyes would see the word "Plantation" plastered as the name of so many housing communities. Again, I wondered is it just me the only one who seems to be bothered by this "plantation thing", because in this decade I would not think this name would be plastered on anything. It was obvious to me that this word never left my consciousness because immediately seeing it bothered me and stirred up mixed emotions. Emotions that would not cease especially when my eyes would see what they would see when I started working a new job opportunity. My reflection again about storms is after the storm some things you just don't see coming. My initial prayers, after my biggest storm yet, was a prayer for a job with less stress, less travel time to and from work, and allow me to be close to my daughters school. My wish for all request were granted and much more again, I received insight into my new destiny. What I would see re-awakened the activist in me.

It all came together, the exact date July 29, 2019 is the day I ended up on todays "Plantation" my thoughts were… "they hire us, yes they do but at the lowest of wage that keeps us economically enslaved". This new job was more than what I anticipated it was the beginning of a new writers destination.

It awakened the activists in me to pursue RACIAL INQUALITY.

It all came together….my conclusion is " a storm just may be leading YOU to a new purposeful destination. Opportunities unseen we must trust and believe. All along it may look like a "setback" but is actually a "setup" storms force us out of our comfort zones and into our purpose zones that otherwise may remain unknown.

My final words about STORMS remember they are disguised as SETBACKS

Storms are not like accidents (accidents unexpectedly happen). A storm is forecasted, (we know it's going to happen). We may not know the exact time but we have a general idea it is on its way well before it arrives! Brace yourself, the storm is coming, be ready so after the storm you are prepared to gather what is of value, what you TRULY need to survive, let go of the muck that will keep you stuck. Listen to that voice that inner guide that is leading you to a new purposeful life.

You must have "Faith" that after the storm you are being led to a purposeful destination!

I'm ready to walk in my purposeful destination

Real Life EXPERIENCE from $80,000 a Year to $16 an Hour

"Nothing becomes real until it is EXPERIENCED"
John Keats

Be careful what you pray for because your prayers just might get answered. I indeed prayed for less stress in my life following my divorce. The drama of that story was taking its toll on me and I knew I needed a change or myself make changes. I had no idea that my request for change would lead me to the "Plantation of Minimum Wage", in other words PLANTATION NATION. I literally went from an $80,000 a year salary to $16 an hour. I prayed for less stress not more stress, my first thoughts, how am I going to survive making only $16 an hour? I immediately asked, "Lord" how did I end up on this journey? How is it that I am middle aged and not getting paid? How can I possible be working at the bottom for a wage that barely allows me to live above poverty. What wrong turns or decisions did I make? My ego was steady talking and getting the best of me and would not stop asking "how can such a thing be, over and over in my brain, how can a smart, experienced middle aged end up on a job making minimum wage"? This is a real life story of how I truly wasn't feeling Gods glory when I had to accept a wage that could keep me enslaved. The cliché of life being a journey…some roads I traveled I specifically chose and some roads I simply did not know, some roads I prayed for direction but this road I could not have ever imagined!

My journey to this modern day "plantation" in hindsight was simply seeing the word many, many years ago and it seemed to bother only me that it was plastered as the name of so many things. As a young 'in I thought I knew the journey and had taken the right roads. Quite frankly I thought I knew it all! Oh, but LIFE has a way of teaching you and I learned LIFE IS LEARNED, there is no way around it….. you learn, you learn, and you learn. I believe this is why we are granted so many years of life. Each day we are blessed to breath is given in pursuit of LEARNING to become the person we are to purposed to become. A life principle I think I am just now starting to grasp LIFE IS A JOURNEY OF LEARNED EXPERIENCES that directs our behaviors and outcomes. One outcome I never saw coming as part of my sunny destination was that I would end up on a modern day plantation. This outcome led to deep soul searching and to ask even more questions why?

For example, why am I here? Why have I been married twice, twice divorced? Why was I born in America oppose to Africa? Why haven't I completed my education and obtained the coveted degree? Why was I born into what some might call a dysfunctional family? Why, why, why? Lord why? Most perplexing of all is why I have been on this road for this long? A journey where before now I could not conceive of institutional racism. I could only conclude that LIFE has its way of getting us were we are supposed to be when we are supposed to be there!

Suddenly there I was! Initially, I sit in secret, I observe, I listen, my EGO again talking to me! As I look around and observe my surroundings it is as blatant as can be the inequities that plague our society. Literally, as far as my eyes could see there was the BROWN SEA. Those working at the lowest level of the work force were the brown skinned people and at the highest level sitting in the offices were the white skinned community. My eyes seeing this sea of beautiful brown skinned people literally blew my mind. It starts me to thinking has it always been this way? Why is it that the eyes of my youth did not see what my middle age eyes of today see which is blatant racism all around me. Repetitive thoughts won't leave my head "Lord am I the only one who sees the inequity of this corporate culture and what looks like to me a modern day plantation"? My conclusion, they hire us, yes they do, but at the lowest of wage that keeps us enslaved! I look around simply puzzled by what I see and the brown skinned people there are just as content as can be. The mind conditioning of this society is something else it leads us to believe in the normalcy of white supremacy. An epiphany for me is what you SEE becomes "normality" it's evident we've all become zombified! Still battling with my thoughts I wonder why and what the heck am I doing here? My EGO unrelenting and getting the best of me say'in "I'm used to a higher wage and I expect to get paid, after all I have many, many years of experience in the health insurance arena so much in fact I can tout myself an expert"! Expert was more like "Sherbert", because "Expert" once a proud mantra of mine became laughable because I ended up in an environment for which I had to become truly adaptable. I talked to myself and wrestled for days trying to make sense of what I was suddenly enthralled in, an archaic environment I would see with my own two eyes. Lord how and why did I end up here? Those unwavering why questions won't leave my head... The journey from an $80,000 a year salary to $16 hourly.

Epiphany, Epiphany, Epiphany! It suddenly occurred to my brain... I had to feel the pain of being undervalued and underpaid. I had to see it and experience it, in order to get it!

Although try as we may we can be totally clueless unless we go through "it" and experience the "PAIN".

For example:

I did not understand the delirium of the broken hearted until I was suddenly broken hearted and alone after my divorce. I experienced the "PAIN" and could truly relate to the lyrics of an "Achy Breaky Heart"!

I could truly sympathize with the sick wanting to quit and surrender life after being struck with sickness myself where I was not getting better and was in physical pain day after day. I no longer wanted to feel the "PAIN" I simply wanted to die!

I so get the grip of grief and the "PAIN" of loss after one of my best friends suddenly passed away. Giggling as we often did I never imagined her passing as a young'in. In my mind we would be giggling until the end of time. I thought she would be here on planet earth with me my entire life!

I was ignorant of the financial struggles of others and the "PAIN" of trying to provide the necessities of life (food and shelter) until I was under paid. The struggle is and was real and I can honestly say that I have been paid a low wage that I was for sure would keep me enslaved!

Experience is the best teacher as you can see, I had to experience it to get it. I learned PAIN and ALL, I had to persevere to carry on. Furthermore, regardless of the emotional turmoil I was experiencing in my head I needed strength from the Divine to move forward with life.

Again, this LIFE OF LEARNING has its way of teaching us what we need to learn. It has its way of leading us where we need to be because cause quite frankly just like the Israelites "we are a stubborn people"! Daily God gives us all opportunities to learn this life and what we are to make of it. In other words the big and the little of why we are here. The song constant in my head over the years, "girl God is trying to tell you something"! I had become distant from my people. I had arrived on the other side I was in the upper middle class. I had been on a respite from the plantation… somehow I thought the racist systems did not apply to me!

But I soon found out when I went from a $80,000 salary to barely making a dollar above the minimum wage that I was not exempt from these systems, the universe was reminding me that I too come from generational poverty. I had to feel the "PAIN" in order to inspire change.

At a higher wage I was EGO tripping and was far removed from my brown skinned people. I had a smooze of elite attitude. I too brought into the lies plastered right before my eyes. The mantra of "Equal Opportunity for All" so eloquently sold it has duped millions to believe there is "Equality" when in fact it is "White Supremacy". The true reality is there is NO EQUAL with history where you have a people who start out from behind because they have been in the rears for at least 157 years. The Emancipation Proclamation of 1863, the official law that set brown skinned folks free seems to be only on paper if you take a look at this nation.

Once more, sometimes we've got to go through it to get it and to really understand the pain of others. I was lead to this journey not simply to be in pain but to actually inspire change of systems that have been in place for decades. God's word assures us that our pain is his gain because "all things work out for the good of those that love him, those who are called according to his purpose", Romans 8:28.

I started to think about my specific prayers before I arrived at the inspiration station.

My specific prayers to reset and recharge my life after 18 years of being in the comfort zone of marital financial security suddenly I was alone dealing with financial obscurity.

My new prayers Lord, I need….

"a Job with a convenient location that allows me to be close to home and close to my daughters school"

"Lord I need a position that allows me to continue to work on those things you have placed in me"
"

Lord you know I have this burning desire to help my people to be the best they can be and to encourage them to do what you have called them to do"

"Lord my latest dream and ask is to be in be in sunny Florida writing on the beach"

"Lord, quite frankly, I need something to live for"!

I repeat be careful what you ask for. I got exactly what I prayed for and more! Attitude turned into gratitude. I had no idea that my journey to this modern day planation would allow me to write a book to inspire a nation. My pain would not be in vain, I was not made to suffer and do nothing, but to feel the "PAIN" and do something! I began to understand this journey for which I was entrenched was not just for me but a stepping stone that would become my testimony for which I could speak and motivate masses and future generations from being paid a wage that could keep them enslaved.

I had to be in it, to get it! I had to feel the pain of being undervalued and underpaid! I had to be reminded because obviously I had forgotten that the blood running through my veins was that of my ancestors who were before me, just like me, born into poverty. Now I could relate and not only change my destiny but the destiny of those economically enslaved from generation to generation.

When I was of the upper middle class I too viewed the struggles of others as their own issues, but I must admit that something would often tug at me. I could never seem to articulate that something was missing in my life and why I felt a disconnect from people just like me born into poverty. Often the thought would come to me why do we leave our brown skinned sisters and brothers behind to fend for themselves? The blind leading the blind in a society that is set in favor of the white skinned kind? And we wonder why they are so troubled? We have to teach our children to help each other not fight each other. How can we expect them to change that which they have no clue, the junk that is being blasted to them too! They too are taught to believe that they have "Equal Opportunity" in this lopsided society which is a "Setup of Systems" based on your skin color is designed to help one skin color over all others. This is a deceptive system that leads masses to believe that they too have a fair shot at this "Equality Thing" and to live the American Dream. The truth is if you are brown skinned in America you may get it, and live it but there won't be any "Equal Opportunity" assisting you to get there! You will get there due to your own sheer will persistence, and determination!

Trust me I had reservation about a writing a book on race relations, especially since I was created to love all people, but the inequities I see with my mature eyes simply bother me. I reflect on the eyes of my youth which a lot they did not conceive or see. The eyes of my youth were the "I/me" eyes because the mind of your youth lives by what it sees and youth thinks it's going to live for eternity. Today I'm thankful for mature eyes and the mind of maturity because it knows death is inevitable this mindset is "what are your going to do for others"!

So, I ask the Divine for guidance to write to inspire the change of "Systems" that have been in place for decades. The system can stagnant a race and keep them enslaved simply because of the low wage it pays.

It saddens me to see so many brilliant brown skinned individuals stuck in a system of blatant racism, and to see the perpetual poverty passed from generation to generation.

As I write this my exact thought is "am I too optimistic"? Is rising above poverty a true reality when the racial disparities have been in place for decades?

I've always believed that I was like the little engine that could, I really never thought about racism and it negatively affecting me because I knew from a young age that God gifted me with intelligence and I have always believed that if others can accomplish their goals and dreams than so can I.

I learned it is only through our learned experiences to which we can speak!

You are created for greatness this you must trust and believe. I have the audacity to believe we all born to accomplish great things. I had to have this journey so that I could get it!

So back to this being a book of inspiration to in fact inspire a nation.

For sure I could not conceive that little ole me was being prepared for bigger things. I leave you with…Sometimes there is no specific road map, you just have to hop on the road to see where it goes. You have to experience it, to get it! You have to trust your arrival to your final destination, you may have been born and purposely put on this road to dismantle PLANTATION NATION!

S.O.S.
Systems of Stagnation

"Your life does not get better by chance,
it gets better by change."
Jim Rohn

Out of sight, out of mind is not just a cliché it is a fact.
It was not until I experienced 1st hand the S.O.S distress
call of today that I have termed "Systems of Stagnation" it
is the virtual plantation of today a system that is designed
to keep brown skinned people economically down. This
was a hard pill to swallow for a middle aged woman of my
caliber working a job paying a wage that I hadn't received
in decades. I now get that I had to experience it in order to
write about " it". It being the " Systems of Stagnation" that
passes poverty from generation to generation.

Life has a way of changing on you and unforeseen life
events can either lead to triumph or tragedy. My life and
income drastically changed after my divorce of 18 years
and it was not until I had to take a job, any job that would
allow me to continue to live and eat that opened my eyes
to a different reality. For many years, sitting in comfort,
I had been at the top of the pay scale I had no clue what
others went through when it came to getting a job. Oh
but life with its constant flow of the unforeseen. It is a new
technological world and with this the trajectory of the job
hunt has changed. The Internet, unforeseen controls just

about everything and it is one of the main systems of today that keeps many economically enslaved. Today's job hunt is virtually controlled by the unknown and this allows for discreet perpetuation of racial discrimination. The powers that be don't have to see you eliminate you. The process of deliberate elimination starts with one question and that is do you have a DEGREE? If no, good luck to you especially if you have brown skin. My resume with the experience so detailed on it, this alone I thought would be a good sell to any employer. To my astonishment it was not. I received little if no response at all. As I began this new life journey in the state of "sunny Florida" which I must add, again, was life without a husband and extra income. My mood soon turned sour as I realized my resume had very little power. The one thing they could use right off to eliminate me, I don't have the completion of a 4 year collegiate education and to add to my job hunt pain was the fact that I am middle AGED!

Nonetheless, I strive to remain of positive mindset and I do believe that life is constantly leading us to where we are supposed to be. I had to eat so I took a job that I consider beneath my abilities. And when I arrived my eyes could not believe what they would see. It was not until I could SEE them because I was now one of them, that I could truly relate to them. The sea of brown people, myself included, at the bottom of the pay scale working a wage, my mind whispered "that truly enslaves". When the epiphany hit my brain, I unknowingly ended up working in a place that I considered upon sight the "modern day plantation". It now made sense why seeing the word "Plantation" many years ago bothered me so. This job that I considered beneath me allowed me to SEE that this is an issue bigger than me. I now had firsthand information regarding these "Systems of Stagnation".

I believe I was being prepared for this journey all along because I too was born into poverty. But as an adult I never really thought about "Generational Poverty" because I was able to work my way up the pay scale and out of it. And when you leave others behind, like I mentioned earlier, "It is out of sight and out of mind". It was not until I could see them that I had remembrance of them. I cannot answer why or what is it about the human psyche that we tend to "FORGET" or "IGNORE" things that we don't actually see or experience. But "life experience" the great teacher that it is allowed me to see them, experience them and most importantly reminded me I AM ONE OF THEM!

"Generational Poverty" or "GP" a term that I personally don't remember we sat around the dinner table discussing. Heck I don't even think it has really been discussed in detail with my inner circle of friends. I cannot even tell you why I had not really thought about it before now as something being passed from one generation to the next. This phase of my life, this middle age phase sees and hears EVERYTHING differently! And it knows some things for certain and wants to communicate with YOU, especially if you are a young person reading this, HEAR ME LOUD AND CLEAR " that if your mama and papa were born to poverty and when they had YOU, you were born into poverty too and the chances of you escaping poverty is pretty slim because again, your mama and papa cannot teach you what they do not know". Remember "GP" is what it specifically says it is "GENERATIONAL POVERTY" so forgive your parents now, it's not their fault! I must repeat this…YOUR PARENTS, AUNTIES, UNCLES, COUSINS, FRIENDS CANNOT TEACH YOU WHAT THEY DON'T KNOW. Life with all its twist and turns was teaching me and leading me exactly where it wanted me to be and when I ended up on today's plantation this journey made so much more sense to me.

I just had to get busy, writing, plotting and planning on how to share what I have learned about the S.O.S distress call of today that I have termed "Systems of Stagnation" that I define as systems designed to keep a brown skinned brother and sister economically down.

I personally could not sit by any longer and do nothing and not prepare future generations properly. For they too will be told that a "white college education" is the way to go for it is the only way to get a good job for which the "white man sits at the controls". True this is the case to be because the white man controls just about everything in this white society. This is the eye of enlightenment for which most of us have not been taught to see that if we abide by the systems then stuck on the plantation we will be. Producing what the white man has implemented while he becomes richer and we become stagnant or poorer and we start to believe that we cannot be more. This is a lie you see planted by the enemy because God created you and me with brains of creativity. We can create whatever our minds conceive. Our great God has gifted us all and we can proudly stand tall and be who he designed us to be and not stay in "Systems of Stagnation" that exist throughout this nation. This is why this this a book on inspiration, my desire is to inspire you so you don't succumb to what this nation desires of you which to remain a working class slave.

It is the "Systems of Stagnation" and my eyes being open to life on the Plantation that lead me to write this book for future generations. I and many others around my age grow up during a time when we as a people coming off the backs of the "Civil Rights" movement. Life for the most part improved for many of us, as we started to experience better lives through obtaining an education. Education supposedly was and still is the "KEY to one's Golden Future". Yes this is the case if one is white because this system has and always will support the generational opportunities of those born of the "white skin". What our parents or care givers failed to tell us and properly prepare us for is this system of "Golden opportunity through education" is just that a "System". It is a system that is controlled by the powers that be which is that of "white supremacy". For generations it has been a system that supports its own first and grants opportunities here and there for others who are willing to work and buy into its systems of bull and shit. I too had and have been bamboozled by its talk of "Equality". I too believed the hype of these words constantly tooted toward me supposedly "Equal Opportunity Society". Their exact words "we do not discriminate" words that I now see in a context so laughable because they are blatant lies that allow a "System of Systems to continually thrive. It works for a few you see but leaves masses of people discombobulated and in a lower class stuck in poverty. This almost happen to me because I started to focus on the struggles of paying bills instead of the greatness I knew God my creator planted within me. So quietly I sit, I watch, I observe, I question what the heck am I a smart middle aged women doing at a minimum wage job? The revelation came that I too am on the "Plantation of Minimum Wage". What a revelation to behold as the story unfolds injustice's to the 10th degree for which my eyes were opened to see. I had to experience it, to get it! They hire us yes they do but at the lowest of minimum wage and my conclusion to keep one a working class slave. This only clicked for me when my eyes could see the masses of us at the bottom of pay for jobs we were hired to daily part take. Then it occurred to me that not only insurance claims specialist were being paid the lowest of wage, but whenever I would call any type of customer service call center I was and would surely be talking to a person of color. This a fact I would not have paid attention to or known if I had not been in a position to experience it on my own! When I looked around at what my eyes would see, blatant racism and a new economy, the economy of minimum wage will keep them a working class slave. This I could only see when the opportunity was afforded me. I had to go backwards before forward so that I could SEE IT for myself, my eyes could testify. I truly believe that I was lead to see to help people who look like me escape "Generational Poverty".

You see when I was at the top of the wage scale just like many others I too forgot the plight of many others and I too bought into the fairy tale of " Equal Rights" propaganda done oh so right because it is plastered on everything you can't help but believe what it intends for you to believe which is "Equal Opportunities for all" this lie is the biggest of ALL. You see this system provides jobs to the masses, but wealth to certain "white" classes. The white elite continue to control there is no denying even today its strong hold.

Again epiphany, epiphany, epiphany, I had to go back so that I could see with my own eyes the blatant racism of this "PLANTATION NATION. "

Generational Poverty must cease! America with its abundant blessings shouldn't provide such a cushy life for some and a sucky life for others. God has blessed this country mightily! It is truly a land that overflows with milk and money! There is more than enough for us all!

Here is the revelation of why we must continue this conversation and stop the atrocities of Generational Poverty.

Even today if brown skin people, those here in this county as descendants of slaves were given 2 acers and a mule (which was the initial promises of one of the founding fathers) there is no way for us to catch up to those who currently rule with so many still economically enslaved to the white man's way. The disparity between the classes are that GREAT! Brown skin people will never, ever catch up this the reality. But if I have my way some things are going to change.

The white man's way, again the S.O.S distress systems of today are all the systems in place that continue to pass generational wealth to the white masses and generational poverty to the brown classes.

Exactly, who or what are these systems? They are our everyday existence of those things we seek and I refer to them as the S.C.C.! Yes, the S.C.C. (Schools, Colleges, Corporations) and just about every other white owned system you can think of.

Thankfully, there are some genuine, God fearing for REAL, loving white skinned people in these systems because if not brown people of color born into poverty in this society really don't stand a chance of upward mobility within these establishments.

I too like many others have been fooled into believing there is "Equal Opportunity" within this society and have bought into this rhetoric that this society sells. I too see the successes of many brown skinned people and think that we have arrived like we are REALLY doing something.

The truth of the matter is only a handful of brown people have broken into and through these systems. Ironically we as a community can literally count them on our hands. Sure we have made strides as a people this I don't deny. My point is when we see the successes in the arenas of sports and entertainment we get blinded by all the glitz and glamour and think we have done something really grand and the truth of the matter is a few of us truly make it and rise above Generational Poverty and most of us "FAKE" it by dressing the outside to the nine's. We "po" but the best dressed kids on the block!

It is evident today, just look around a few of us making it has literally done "NOTHING" to truly penetrate these systems. The needle that represents brown people of color that remain in poverty literal has not moved. We started at the bottom, year 1619, 400 years ago when the first slaves were brought to this country and 157 Years of FREEDOM we still here, at the bottom!

A brief summary since being set FREE 157 years ago:

From year 1863 – until present year 2020 = 157 Years of FREEDOM, *prosperity for some brown people of color but the bottom is still the reality for the masses!*

157 Years of being at the bottom:

Year	The Movement	#of Years-Still-No-Change
1863	**The Emancipation Proclamation of 1863** signed by Abraham Lincoln freed all Confederate Slaves.	1 Year at the Bottom
1865	**The 13th Amendment** abolished slavery. Instituted in 1865 it is the official doc that sets us ALL free (Us being people of African Origins with African blood running through our veins).	2 Years at the Bottom
1866	**Civil Rights Act of 1866** – The 1st Official doc that states we too are citizens of the great USA! "The act declares that all persons born in the United States were now citizens, without regard to race, color, or previous condition."	3 Years at the Bottom
1865-1877	**The Reconstruction Years** is this country attempting to get it together and redress the inequities of slavery and its political, social and economic legacy.	14 Years at the Bottom (1863 – 1877)
1877 - 1950	**Jim Crow** – Although FREE the Jim Crow Laws of segregation prohibited the advancement of brown people. Jim Crow laws in 1877. The laws mandated the segregation of public schools, public	87 Years at the Bottom (1863 – 1950)

places, and public transportation, and the segregation of restrooms, restaurants, and drinking fountains for whites and blacks.

The Civil Rights Movement started in the late 1940's, but the official movement is logged as 1954-1968. This movement was an organized effort by black Americans to end racial discrimination and gain equal rights under the law. The fight was for civil rights equal to those of whites, including equal opportunity in employment, housing, and education, as well as the right to vote, and the right of equal access to public facilities. The Civil Rights Act of 1964 was the result of this movement. It is the official law of the USA that bands discrimination based on race, color, religion, sex, or national origin. It prohibits unequal application of voter registration requirements, and racial segregation in schools, employment, and public accommodations.

105 Years at the bottom (1863 – 1968)

This movement and the Civil Rights Act of 1964 was thought to be the change necessary for the advancement of people of color. It did help some, but not the masses of those born into the Generational Poverty. People of color are born behind and it is almost impossible to rise above the poverty line with "Systems of Stagnation" in place today that stems from the plantation of yesterday. The ugliness of slavery is still a present day issue 157 years after the Emancipation Proclamation of 1863 setting us FREE.

1969 - 2020

No official new laws or movements for the Advancement of People of color. Life for those born into Generational Poverty work low wage jobs, experience high black on black crime, drug use, prostitution, robbery, murder of one's own including children, and every evil act of sin that one can think of in their neighborhoods. This population of US citizens are virtually left in their neighborhoods to fend for themselves. There is talk about "it" but not much is done about "it"! Nothing of significance has changed.

157 Years at the bottom
(1863 – 2020)

My conclusion is its time for a new movement, a FOR REAL movement that will squelch the Generational Poverty that ultimately keeps masses of brown skinned people stuck at the bottom economically of such a thriving society.

A "157 Year history" fascinating to me because as I write this, I am 53 and to think that I have been on this planet 53 years and not really much has changed I find fascinating! I had no idea I would write such a book, PLANTATION NATION, The Inspiration YOU Need to Break FREE. One Hundred and Fifty-Seven Years of FREEDOM, yet 400 years since slavery and this is the true reality. Just because we are FREE the powers that be didn't change much of anything.

Hooked Winked and Bamboozled is what continues to happen in this thriving society of "systems" that supports the advancement of white skinned people, not all people. People of color, YES, YES, YES we have made strides, we have more kids going to college, some of us climb the corporate ladder, some of us own successful businesses... yet the economy of today keeps many economically enslaved. We as a people have been free for 157 years and counting, still the needle has not moved we have literally been running on the same road in the same place. Wow! What a revelation, imagine you have been on the same road in the same place for 157 years. Many of us are just tired! No wonder why so many suffer from serious illnesses and have the high rates of diabetes, high blood pressure, heart attacks, and mental illness that is rampant in brown skinned communities. We are tired because we have been running on the same road! This road has been an avenue for a few, some are able to move on and up the road to opportunity and out of poverty   maneuvering like Mohamad Ali bobbing and weaving through a matrix of systems designed to support again, one race and not all races. These "Systems of Stagnation" allow for the mobility of movement for some to " move on down the road" resulting in a few that move into better economic situations… they good….they got their food, shelter and material things. They don't have to be concerned about the rest of us because they are so far removed from us that they don't even remember us. Yes 'us" because I now work and receive a wage that would keep me a working class slave. They too like me have been fooled / hoodwinked and bamboozled into thinking …."Equal Opportunity"!

They say, "just work hard and believe and you too can accomplish your dreams." Now this I do wholeheartedly believe it's just that there is no such thing as "Equal Opportunity" in this lopsided society. There is blatant discrimination across this great nation.

It bothers me tremendously now that my eyes have been opened and I see what I see. A smart loving people stuck in struggle and reluctant to dream because of the existing "Systems of Stagnation" that keep masses stuck on the existing "working class plantation". I cannot say it enough "The Plantation of Minimum Wage" that keep masses of brown skinned people economically enslaved.

Again, the successes of a few did and does not cause the needle to move. Oprah Winfrey, Tyler Perry, Beyoncé, and the Obamas can't save a race all by themselves! It will take the efforts of all of us to truly move many of us down the road of opportunity into the striving, thriving people that God has created us to be.

In conclusion, many have moved on down the road and suffer from amnesia and have truly forgotten the pain that our ancestors endured for our gain. The stench of slavery is a distant memory in most minds so we believe we are free and have "Equal Opportunity". We have forgotten about

the slave trade that had us enslaved and many refuse to believe this is the case of today. Today there are no physical chains, but the low "wage paid" undoubtedly keeps us is virtual chains. We don't see them, but there are there.
It wasn't until I took a job way below my skill set that I could plainly see with my own two eyes. My eyes were wide open to the inequality that still exist in this society. It wasn't until I could SEE them and was reminded...I AM ONE OF THEM! I'm at the bottom of the pay scale. Like a brick it hit my mind I'm in a system designed to keep a people behind.

I picked up my pen and I began to write..... about the "Plantation of Minimum Wage" an economic system that perpetuates Generational Poverty, concluding this is still a PLANTATION NATION. Sure they hire us but at the minimalist amount of wage that keeps masses of brown skinned people economically enslaved!

157 Years of FREEDOM and being at the bottom of the US Economy, a *history like no other! But like the Egyptians I amazed that 400 years later many of us are still enslaved.*

The Crap Crasher
Corporate CRAP Spewed across
PLANTATION NATION

"The B.S. that Keeps People Economically
Enslaved on the Plantation"

As to who I am I hate crap period. Tell me the truth or tell me nothing at all. Truth the genetic code I inherited from my mama to whom I could only speak truth because if you lied you would face her wrath undenied. I've deemed myself the "Corp Crap Crasher" because just like my mama I have zero tolerance for blatant lies. I personally can no longer tolerate it, the "CRAP" that is spewed across this nation, especially the catchphrase "Equality" that is plastered and written on so many corporate communications.

The epiphany, the day "Corporate Crap" hit my brain I immediately began to define it as "the lies and the systems put in place to immortalize the success of the white skinned race". It amazes me that it blatantly bamboozles the masses into believing this "Equal Opportunity" slogan. Corporate Crap is something that I had been wrestling with for years but I could not articulate into words, it's only now that I am able to discern. I say wrestle because

I so want to believe we are truly an "Equal Opportunity Society". My reality is so many times I have applied to jobs that I know I was unquestionably qualified, but I would receive rejection after rejection and this is when I started to question the systems in place that stop me right out the gate because more times than not I was interviewed by someone white. What my life's journey to date has taught me is that "Equal" can never be when a predominate race has for centuries controlled everything. Here are just a few slogans that sucker us all in and they might as well include the word "white". The truth is we live in a world of white domination, that tricks you to believe what it wants you to believe and that is that we live in a world of "Equal Opportunity".

We've all bought into the headlines:

Their words say....	What they should say....
"Join Our Team"	"Join Our Team" "especially if you are white"
"Career Opportunities"	"Career Opportunities" "for white educated communities"
"Now Hiring Talented Individuals"	"Now Hiring Talented white Individuals"
"Our Benefits are Top of the Line"	"Our Benefits are Top of the Line for white individuals"
" Your life. Your *career*"	" Your white life. Your white *career*"
" Who we are – explore the stories behind our diverse workforce"	" Who we are – explore the stories behind our diverse predominately white elite workforce"
"We bring amazing people together to make amazing things happen"	"We bring amazing white people together to make amazing things happen"

Proudly they post and boast of these headlines but what they fail to say is that we are dealing with generations and generations of "White" policies that have been put into place. Policies designed to perpetuate the domination of white mankind. Policies that lead to generational poverty for brown mankind who are essentially "generational slaves" which is a hard pill to swallow. But, if you are hired at the minimum of wage essentially you are a "generational slave" because you are paid a wage designed to keep you lowest on the pay scale and stuck in struggle that seems like "hell" because it is hard to provide the simple necessities of life. You too have been swindled by the "Equal Opportunity" disclaimer that has duped millions into to the belief that this is an "Equal Opportunity Society".

My discovery is Corporations are the biggest perpetuators of Racial Discrimination today, them with all their rules and regulations, they undoubtedly have systems in place that propels the white skinned race. And the CRAP they spew I can no longer adhere to! It is time to start addressing the truth of the matter which is there is generational wealth for whites at the start of life and there is no way that those who start out behind have fair "Equal Opportunity".

"Equal Opportunity" is a delusion because there are unfair systems in place from the beginning. A system so unfair because if you were born behind in many cases you stay behind due to the starting wage that corporations pay. In addition, generational poverty, can be crippling because more than likely brown skinned individuals don't have the same credentials as their white skinned cohorts and usually no fault of their own because (poverty begets poverty) and in many cases brown skinned individuals cannot afford to seek the education or the "degree" which could give them some upward mobility in this white society.

What I need brown people to know don't fall for the okie doke there is no such thing as "Equal Opportunity" in this society. We have a 400 year history of being behind. Again that means we start out behind and in many cases stay behind. I need you brown skinned to get this in your mind, from the moment we are born many of us not all of us are in the last position. So no matter what slogans they plaster there is no such thing as "Equal Opportunity". It will never be equal when there are generational systems in place that are dominated by the "white skinned race". We all must never forget the generational history we are dealing with. On both sides is the generational tide and it shifts in the direction based on the color of the skin with which you were born. If you are brown skinned your tide leads to poverty and if you are white skinned your tide leads to prosperity. This is the truth but as life goes on we all tend to get amnesia about policies in place set by the predominately wealthy white skinned race. "Out of sight and out of mind", life as usual we all continue to be bamboozled.

As the Corp Crap Crasher, I'm going to remind you over and over there is no such thing as "Equal Opportunity Employment" generational poverty is the harsh reality. As brown skinned continue to get hired at the lowest of wage that keeps them economically enslaved.

Now I'm not saying that there is NO opportunity, trust you me I thank God often that I was born in America behind. Yes I too was born behind, I was born into generational poverty, but again, I'm thankful I was born in the land of the free where I can work as hard as I like and create my own opportunities. My frustration is this society leads masses to believe there is "Equal Employment Opportunity" THERE IS NO SUCH A THING with the current systems in place and wealth disparities where riches lead more to the white skinned race.

"Success begets Success and "Poverty begets Poverty"

I believe that as brown skinned people we have to
prepare our children differently and not set them up or
dup them into to believing there is "Equal Opportunity
Employment." The truth of the matter they will have to
work their butts off in a world that is designed to keep them
behind. Sure some will succeed following the protocol of
today, but you must know there is much more at stake.
Just take a look at black on black crime, we have turned on
each other unlike any other. And I believe it's because we,
yes "WE" including myself have left so many behind in a
world that is not designed for them to individually prosper
and shine.

We have bought into the B.S. that is spewed. Brown
skinned people we must be like the Jewish people and
never ever forget the atrocities suffered specifically to our
kind. We must regroup and stop leaving our brothers and
sisters behind. We have to forgive them because "they
TRULY know not what they do" they are only responding
because they have no clue. We are the only group that
gains success and leave our brothers and sisters behind to
deal with mess they have no clue about how to address
which is you are born in a world that is designed to keep
you behind. **Again, "Poverty begets Poverty", just like
"Success begets Success", my mama, your mama, could
not teach me or you what they themselves did not know**,
like so many others they were only doing what they had
been told and believed the lies that they had been sold
which is to go to college and earn the covenant degree or
join the armed forces. Both of these are great endeavors
to strive for but what they fail to tell you and prepare you
for is you may be the only brown skinned person they have

allowed through the door. You will be in a world where you are outnumbered, possible isolation like no other, you can only be what they allow you to be if you are not confident in who God created you to be and create your own opportunities.

Again "Success begets Success", that being said any of us who has experienced success to any degree must return to the communities from when we come and stop leaving masses behind to fend for themselves in a world that is not designed for them to prosper. For the betterment of mankind we must teach what we have learned and implement the "each one teach one" strategy so our kind will not only know better to do better, but they can actually learn to strategize and rise above the poverty line.

Thank God for role models and others that show us life that on our own we may not discover. I personally had no specific strategy but it only took one person to inspire me higher.

Here is my brief young adult story of how I was inspired to rise above generational poverty...... when I graduated from high school I instinctively knew two things; one I would have to get a job to take care of myself and second I didn't want to end up on the welfare system. Other than these two things, I knew nothing and I had no clue what I wanted to do with my life, my mama could only teach and inspire me so much, with her herself only having only a 9th grade education. Again, intuitively within me my desire to not end up on welfare was strong. I saw the struggles of my family and my people who were on the welfare system and to my young mind at the time it was clear welfare was not for me. Miraculously it registered to my young brain that life on welfare is/was hard. Yes "miraculously" because I didn't know much but somehow I grasped early on that waiting on a monthly check and food stamps was not it. I'm amazed that to date I am the only member of my immediate family who has never been on the welfare system.

Once more, thank God for miracles and role models because there was the one role model for me at a crucial time in my life when I really needed one. Juanita was her name, she was the one person I knew that had a job and appeared to me to have it going on. She had the things that I wanted that being on welfare would not afford like a car, a house, but most importantly a GOOD job at an insurance company. I wanted what she had so I immediately applied at the insurance company where she worked, I got the job, and at the ripe age of "19" my humble beginnings was that of a medical insurance claims processor and customer service rep. Once I started working I knew being at the bottom of the working class was not for me, again, instinct kicked in. I was starting to learn what I was capable of, something within was whispering to me... "you are smart and can work your way to the top" which I did. I truly winged my way up the so called ladder of success all I knew to do was model everyone else and that modeling was apply for jobs rated at hire positions and move up the pay scale. I've always been brainy and a fast learner so I was able to work my way up and I eventually I landed by dream position as a systems trainer. When we don't know we simply do what we have been taught or told. Remember my mama couldn't teach me what she herself did not know so even though I worked my way up the ladder I had no other goals. I enrolled in college just like everybody else but other than that because I had to figure so many things out on my own I had no clue what a degree would do and that is holding this piece of paper could prevent me from being paid a wage that could keep me economically enslaved. The irony of this brief story is I have been in the insurance world 25 plus years, my entire work life and I'm amazed that as I write this book I'm literally working at a wage that I earned over two decades ago. I've come to know by my own experience there are systems in place that automatically knock you out of the race to be paid the income you have rightfully earned. The reality today is if you are brown skinned and don't have the credentials to match your white skinned compadres (more than likely they will have a collegiate degree, the systems are in their favor) good luck to you aspiring to avoid working at a wage that won't keep you a working class slave. Many of us, yes me too, simply have to suck it up and take a job any job to eat and keep our lights on.

Now back to corporations and the roles they play in keeping browned skinned people economically enslaved. Again I have deemed myself the "Corporate Crap Crasher" and I therefore have to define the word "CRAP" before I go any further to give you an understanding of the bull and shit we are under.

CRAP as defined by Dictionary.com -

Nonsense, falsehood, exaggeration, propaganda, rubbish, junk, baloney, foolishness, hogwash, ridiculousness, rigamarole, tomfoolery, ludicrousness

I'm so bothered by the "Corporate Crap" that is spewed across this PLANTATION NATION and this book is my way to fight back. I can no longer engage in a muted racial debate while BIG corporations hide behind their propaganda of published lies and they still have systems in place that continue to "propel" the white skinned race. Since my work back ground is health insurance here is the CRAP talk of three top companies who have basically done nothing but talk a good game for which this society is being played. In every office across this nation at the executive level I guarantee you will see a "White" skinned executive that is the lead. Usually there is 1 token or a few persons of color to represent the "Equality" to which these corporations speak. They will lead you to believe they are about true diversity and as I speak of them I have purposely removed their names. They may be different companies but I found they are all the same, the bottom line is it doesn't matter specifically who they are they are ran by generations of the white skinned that implement the same policies. From what I can see it is about maintaining control and GREED because they continue to make BILLIONS while literally economically enslaving millions. Again, they talk a good game but they have no interest in changing a wage that keeps masses a working class slave.

Slogans of 3 Top Insurance Corporations (Diversity & Inclusion Clauses) as reported on their websites, revenue captured from Google:

Company "A" – Revenue USD (2019): 242.2 Billion

19 Executive Leaders, (18 White, 1 Black)

Diversity creates a healthier atmosphere…..

Inclusion & Diversity

We come from a variety of backgrounds and experiences, and recognize that when we all come together the power of each of us is magnified. Culture, inclusion and diversity councils are role models for our diverse workforce and champion inclusive strategies to drive value and impact.

Equal Opportunity and Affirmative Action / "Equal Opportunity Employment is The Law"

To maintain a workplace that accepts and appreciates the differences among our employees. The company will not discriminate against any applicant or employee based on age, race, gender, color, religion, national origin, ancestry, disability, marital status, covered veteran status, sexual orientation, gender identity and/or expression, status with respect to public assistance or any other characteristic protected by state, federal, or local law.

Company "B" – Revenue USD (2018): 92.11 Billion
8 Executive Leaders (7 White, 1 Back)

Workforce Diversity

We believe that having a diverse workforce is critical to innovation and to addressing the needs of the diverse customers and communities we serve. Women make up 76% of our workforce and 63% of all management roles. People of color represent 43% of our workforce and 29% of management.

Inclusion and Diversity

Our inclusive culture is essential to attracting talent that understands and connects with our consumers.

Nondiscrimination Notice - It's important we treat you fairly That's why we follow federal civil rights laws in our health programs and activities. We don't discriminate, exclude people, or treat them differently on the basis of race, color, national origin, sex, age, or disability.

"EEO is the Law"

Equal Opportunity Employer

EEO Policy Statement (a link to this specific policy)

Company "C" – Revenue USD (2018): 195 Billion

10 Executive Leaders, (All White)

Diversity

*** serves millions of people every day. For our company to thrive, it's important to have a workforce that reflects not only our customers, but also the communities they live in.

Celebrating over 300k diverse employees

Diversity touches every aspect of our business. Every day we seek out and implement new solutions from colleagues from all walks of life. We believe that for our business to thrive, our workforce must reflect the diversity of the communities we serve. And all of our colleagues must feel empowered to succeed. We work hard to foster a diverse and inclusive workplace, accepting of all employees who bring unique perspectives.

We are committed to maintaining a diverse and inclusive workplace.

An equal opportunity and affirmative action employer. We do not discriminate in recruiting, hiring or promotion based on race, ethnicity, gender, gender identity, age, disability or protected veteran status. We comply with the laws and regulations set forth in the following...

EEO is the Law Poster: EEO IS THE LAW and EEO IS THE LAW SUPPLEMENT.

Equal Opportunity/Affirmative Action employer. Gender/ Ethnicity/Disability/Protected Veteran – we highly value and are committed to all forms of diversity in the workplace...

Again I must speak on this "Equal Opportunity Employment is The Law" clause, I'm going to state it over and over, there is "No Equal" "Poverty begets Poverty" and "Success begets Success" many brown skinned people have to take whatever job they can get and in many instances it is starting at the lowest of wage that will keep them economically enslaved. As I got into writing this book one day it dawned on me that whenever I would call a customer service call center, no matter what type of business, i.e. cable, utilities, insurance, the post office. It did not matter when or what time I called, in most cases a browned skinned person answered the call.

The starting pay for a Customer Service Representative can range from ($13 - $18 an hour). The Starting pay has got to change to match the cost of living of today, if not the starting pay is keeping people economically enslaved right out the gate.

Official data from the Bureau of Labor Statistics:

The median hourly wage for customer service representatives was $16.23 in May 2018. The median wage is the wage at which half the workers in an occupation earned more than that amount and half earned less. The lowest 10 percent earned less than $10.65, and the highest 10 percent earned more than $26.59. Last Modified Date: Wednesday, September 4, 2019.

https://www.bls.gov/ooh/office-and-administrative-support/customer-service-representatives.htm#tab-5

I argue that is the "Corporation" that is ultimately responsible for the stagnation and the systems in place that keep a brown skinned people economically enslaved by paying a minimum wage.

If you are an executive of a corporation I know that you personally may not be a racist and I personally don't blame you but I do need for you to know that you are responsible for the generational strongholds that keep systems in place that perpetuate benefits for the "white skinned" race. If you truly want to make this world a place of "Equality" then it is your responsibility to implement real change by removing moot systems and by paying a starting wage that won't keep people economically enslaved.

Top executives this is the "Corporate CRAP" I'm tired of and can no longer stomach... .Global Responsibility, Social Responsibility and Diversity clauses... the words YOU boast when in actual numbers you haven't done much of nothing but have perpetuated the same decade after decade.

The truth of the matter is until your BILLIONS have re-set the course of millions born into poverty especially when you have profited from this population, you should be embarrassed to speak about the very little you have done, for example:

Company "B" mentioned above proudly boast – in 2015 we joined the United Negro College Fund Corporate Scholar Program providing scholarships, internships and mentoring for rising college juniors, seniors and graduate students of various cultural and ethnic backgrounds. Company "B" continues to boast they have " already awarded 15 Academic Scholarships and has offered SDIP Internships to 12 students". This is nothing to boast about but quite frankly to laugh about.

I personally don't get it but I have concluded that corporations must be told...so here you go..."When you are a multi-BILLION dollar company and you boast you have only awarded 15 Academic scholarships and SDIP internship to 12 students YOU should be ashamed of your Corporate Self! This is nothing to brag about or even mention. Please don't post or boast until YOU have provided Academic Scholarships of ...1500, 15,000 150,000 or Internships of ....1200, 12,000, 120,000 or even more to the underserved communities from which you make a portion of your BILLION DOLLAR Revenues. Essentially many of you "corporations" are pimping the population because you underpay the brown skinned people, and you make much money off of them, their underserved friends, and family members who are on MEDICAID. Yes I snitch! As the "Crap Crasher" I know that many do not know of this revenue generating cycle. I repeat in street talk, YOU BIG PIMP'IN because you make a lot of money from the population you underpay that keeps them a working class slave. Ironically the starting pay is so low they themselves in many cases may have to apply for MEDICAID, the flagitious cycle continues.

More CRAP proudly displayed by Company "B" -
Our Sales Diversity Internship Program (SDIP) focuses on improving the racial diversity of our workforce by offering students experiences to develop critical sales skills. Since it began in 2012, SDIP has hosted 41 ethnically diverse interns and hired 16 for full-time positions.

Again I cannot stomach it, host 41 and hired 16, for REAL this is laughable, I'm embarrassed for you. If you are going to Boast of what you do to help the community – DO SOMETHING FOR REAL to create a real diverse workforce that represents "Equality" and eliminate the current systems that prevent the change necessary to propel these numbers to shift higher!

The real kicker – the BOAST that did me in is when I discovered this article online written and published November 10, 2015 by Southern New Hampshire University, CFA Staff, Case Studies, about a specific company. Pay close attention to the bolded items below and as you read them include "white people or for white people".

Why Anthem is willing to pay for 51,000 employees to go to college – Southern New Hampshire University "College for America"

https://collegeforamerica.org/why-anthem-is-willing-to-pay-for-51000-employees-to-go-to-college/

One of the nation's largest health benefits companies, Anthem, Inc., is investing in professional development of its workforce in a partnership with the nonprofit College for America at Southern NH University—and now more than 1,000 employees are earning an accredited college degree and positioning themselves for potential promotions. In the last several years, the Affordable Care Act has dramatically shifted the business landscape in the health insurance industry. Today, consumers rather than employers are the primary drivers of business growth. And for healthcare payers, this new customer-centric dynamic has created more competition for skilled workers.

Aimee Skinner, director of learning and development at Anthem, Inc., explained her company's challenge: "Seventy percent of our future growth will come from consumer choice segments whose ideas of customer service are set by their interactions with popular consumer companies like Zappos, TripAdvisor and Uber. That means policyholders have come to expect 24/7 service with personalization and exceptional experiences. Overall, this shift in our business means we need a more educated and skilled workforce to meet customer expectations."

Anthem has affiliated health plans and Medicaid managed care programs in more than 20 US states, and the on-the-ground challenges of local operations mirror the need for national consumer-centric growth. Additionally, Anthem Blue Cross and Blue Shield in New Hampshire (Anthem BCBS) has been facing workforce-related challenges common across corporations nationwide. The demographics of its associates are shifting: the average age of an associate is 49.2 years; average tenure, 14 years; and nearly two out of every three associates work from home. Moreover, it finds that its employees often lack the skills needed for promotion and to strengthen critical thinking skills, writing, analytics, and other soft skills.

And thy might as well add "This is why, we've got to get our white people ready"

Piloting a promising approach

In 2013, Anthem BCBS partnered with the nonprofit, fully accredited College for America at Southern New Hampshire University to pilot a workplace-applicable degree program built specifically for working adults. The program was a good fit for Anthem given its growing need for more-skilled employees—only one-third of them had an associate degree or higher. "From the very first time I heard the College for America concept explained, I was struck by how much sense it made and by how it addressed not only the challenges that working adults face in completing a degree, but also some significant challenges we faced as an employer," explained Lisa Guertin, President of Anthem BCBS. "The decision to participate was really a no-brainer." "From the very first time I heard the College for America concept explained, I was struck by how much sense it made. The decision to participate was really a no-brainer." —Lisa Guertin, President, Anthem Blue Cross and Blue Shield in New Hampshire

Guertin and her team were interested in seeing how the online, competency-based approach would improve skills, engagement, retention and opportunities for advancement. The program's affordability was also a key factor. Like 74% of US employers, Anthem offers its associates tuition assistance for higher education—up to $5,000 annually. While the benefit is generous, it is still quickly used up at a traditional college with high tuition costs, leaving employees to either cover the rest of the tuition bill or take courses over many years. College for America tuition is only $2,500 per year and students learn at a self-directed pace. As a result, Anthem associates can earn a degree at no cost to them and often much faster than through traditional higher education options.

Educational leaps and bounds

Associates were invited into the pilot program in early 2013, and many jumped at the opportunity for higher education that could fit into their busy lives. For example, pursuing a degree had never been much of an option for Starrann Freitas. The single mother of two had poured her energy and spare time into work and raising her boys. So when she was accepted into the associate degree pilot, she didn't waste any time and completed her degree in less than a year. A quick promotion followed, and she decided to continue and earn her bachelor's degree, which she completed in late 2015.

Going nationwide with a proven model

Based on the overwhelmingly positive results of the pilot, Guertin and her team worked with Anthem, Inc. at a national level to expand the College for America associate's and bachelor's degree programs to all eligible 51,000 full-time and part-time associates at no cost to the employees. "The response to the pilot exceeded my expectations, and I knew we were on to something that needed to spread beyond New Hampshire," explained Guertin. Jose Tomas, executive vice president and chief human resources officer (CHRO) at Anthem, Inc., echoed the sentiment: "Our partnership with College for America has proven successful for our associates who participated in the pilot program in New Hampshire and we want to build on that success by providing opportunities for education, development and career advancement to all our associates." In the spring of 2015, College for America and Anthem, Inc. collaborated to develop a nationwide launch plan. In June, Anthem announced the new partnership, first by informing managers about the program and opportunity, and then by encouraging associates to participate via an email from the CHRO, a co-branded web page, printed materials and desktop screen savers. The partnership received additional coverage in mainstream, local, and niche-market media. As of October 2015:

- 10,000 expressed interest
- 3,200 associates applied
- 1,400 associates enrolled
- 18 Anthem students graduated

Aimee Skinner says that, for Anthem, the College for America program represents an investment in associates and the future of the company. "One thing we love about the College for America competency-based approach is that our employees tell us how relevant the learning is to their everyday jobs and lives. We know that the degree projects often closely mirror real-life situations, so the problem-solving and communications skills employees are gaining are directly applicable to their work. It's satisfying to know that our education investments are paying off by helping improve employee lives and the quality of our customer service," concludes Skinner.

I'm just going to drop the PEN!
New Hampshire is 93% white.

Need I say more – this partnership did me in PERPETUATION of the same old thing which is domination of the "white skinned" and the Corporate CRAP that is spewed across this PLANTATION NATION.

Footnote:

The racial makeup of New Hampshire as of the July 2019 Census Bureau, Quick Facts:

White: 93.2% (90% White alone, not-Hispanic or Latino), Black or African American: 1.7%, Hispanic or Latino: 3.9%, Asian alone: 3.0%, American Indian and Alaska Native: 0.3%

Thank GOD
for
the GOOD WHITE PEOPLE

"The Real Change Agents are the people
who care about other human beings"

As I prayed and asked for direction "Lord" how am I
going to write a book on racism when I love all people?
The whispers in my spirit…. it's time for a change and race
relations as they have been will be of the past.

I felt that I was spiritually led to write this chapter
specifically to white people to remind you that you too
have responsibility to make this world a better place by
doing your part to work on race relations. Most of you
have been in your comfort zones for way too long! And you
have no clue as to what to do. Let you not forget your vital
role that is necessary in the change that needs to take place
within the human race. Your job is to work on race and
not spread hate. You can no longer rest on your laurels,
Your world is changing too. Crime affects ALL and the
criminally minded tend to come from generational poverty!
No matter how many gated communities you build crime
will get to you too!

I call upon you to be people who genuinely care about
other human beings and not remain stuck in a place that
perpetuates hate. The truth of the matter is I would not be

where I am today without the "GOOD WHITE PEOPLE" those who looked beyond my brown skin and simply cared for me as a fellow human being. Had it not have been for those/these people, I call "the GOOD WHITE PEOPLE" who came into my community to inspire me and expose me to the finer things in life. I shudder to think what would have become of me.

Today I thank God for those who actually came into my little world of existence these people today remain a memorable force in my mind. They were simply people who truly cared about other people. Thankfully they lived and came outside of their comfort zone (the white zone) so that the love of God might be known.

For example, Sue a missionary who lived in our community. Yes lived within the community. It was because of her that I had the opportunity to see and experience life outside the hood. I remember so vividly the time she took many of us to meet her family. I was a city girl, a.k.a. a hood rat, who grew up around brick and mortar. Before the visit to Sues family's farm the only time my eyes would see green pastures outside of the city neighborhood park was when we would do a literal drive-by. LOL, On occasion as a family we would "drive-by" the plush green lawns of the houses owned by rich white people. Today, I laugh because my young mind thought all white people were rich.

Now I know that all white people aren't rich they have their financial struggles too!

Back to Sue and her family... Arriving at her family's farm I was like wow not just the rich white people but also

the caring white people live in big houses with this plush
green pastures. Because of Sue and her loving family my
experience was not a "drive-by" but I was provided with a
"real life experience" it was an actual stop at a house that
I would not only see rolling acres of green pastures but
I would actually sit it and touch the green lawn my own
hands.

Again, my eyes had only seen green pastures as "drive-by's".
I could not conceive that I would one day walk on them.
The "real life experience" of it and the positive impression
it left on my young mind is why I will never forget it! As
I recall the memory, I am so thankful for "Sue" who was
doing what she was put on this planet to do and that was to
care for and show love to others. Her loving actions made a
tremendous impact on my life, because of her I didn't grow
up so focused on the negativity of racism. I grow up with
the belief that people are innately good!

Once I got over what my eyes would initially see, what I
remembered most was the love I felt from her family.

Sue and her family provided a lasting life impression.
A memory so impactful that even today it is one of my
most cherished childhood memories. My experience with
this family left me with a lasting impression of the "good
white people". It provided me with not only a memory
but something tangible, which lead to life being attainable
and not just a vision in my mind. Here's why, spending
time with this family was like what I had seen on TV
except better because this was a real life experience. I was
an eyewitness to a true loving family and how they interact
with each other. Her dad so reminded me of Santa Claus,
he was FOR REAL a jolly round man just as happy as he
could be. Her mom, now that I think about it was a REAL

Mrs. Clause. She was just as happy as she could be in the kitchen making fresh homemade biscuits for us to eat. I attribute my love for Dolly Parton to this family because this is where my ears first heard her music. Just like in the movies we sat down as a family around a table, talked, laughed and enjoyed the good food!

Lastly, the love that was shown and that was showered upon me is what opened my eyes ...to the goodness of people period...they may have different skin than me, but their heart is no different. The epiphany for me at a young age was there are people in the world who don't have brown skin like me and they really do care about other people. So again I'm thankful because of the "GOOD WHITE PEOPLE" in my life to teach me and show me otherwise, Sue was just one of the many who came into our hood and showed they cared.

Also, there was officer John who would come and play football with us in a playground domain (The Green Lot), and the white camp counselors who came into our hood to expose us to nature by taking us to camp grounds located many miles from the brick and mortar setting we were use to. I must add, my first camp experience I cried like a baby on the 1st day but it soon became one of my favorite life experiences and what I attribute to my current love for nature. Can you see, can you see, I hope that I have written this plainly because of these "GOOD WHITE PEOPLE" I just didn't view "white people" as the enemy, I did not fear them as I do today. I never saw them as a specific hindrances to my life, my mind, my eyes were not so in tuned to the racism I see and encounter today. In my youth my encounters with white people were positive and it's a shame today that I would be hesitant to interact with them, especially police officers for fear that I could lose my life!

This is why I refer to you as the "GOOD WHITE PEOPLE" the "Real Change Agents" of today it is your duty to make this world a better place for future generations. Especially if it is a world that your children are left to live in. The Real Change Agents are the people who care about other human beings.

White skinned people come out of your comfort zones and out of your houses, on the other side of your plush green lawns there is other work for you to do too!

Wise up, mix it up, add some flavor
and do your part to make the world a better place for the
human race.
I am Michelle and this is my mantra

Ignorance is not Bliss it is
IGNORANCE!

They say "ignorance is bliss" and I say "Ignorance is IGNORANCE"!

Ignorance means you are not in the know! It is defined as "lack of knowledge, learning, and information". As I began to delve into the necessary research that should be included in such a book as this I ponder if I have been under a rock or am I just ignorant! Admittedly I have been ignorant regarding systems in place that stagnant a race. Ignorance may be a strong word but it accurately describes the mindset of many minds, "we simply lack knowledge". I'm no lone ranger when it comes to lack of knowledge, here read for yourself the comments of others that describes the lack of knowledge perpetuated from one generation to another.

Comments as reported by Associated Press online article written by Corey Williams and Noreen Nasir, October 25, 2019 – AP-NORC poll: Most American oppose reparations for slavery:

A 79 white woman of West Palm Beach, Florida, opposes cash reparations and an official government apology.

"None of the black people in America today are under the slavery issue," she says, "It's over with."

Using taxpayers' money to pay reparations "would be unfair to me," she added. "My ancestors came to this country, worked hard to become Americans and never asked for anything,"

Not everyone realizes how horrible slavery was to black Americans, said 63-year-old Nathan adding that the federal government should apologize for slavery "because it was wrong."

While he supports reparations, Jordan, who is black and lives in, Georgia, can't put a dollar figure on what would be fair.

"I don't think the government could even afford that," he said. "I don't know what the value would be. There are still a lot of (black) people trying to catch up. I'm not sure if they'll ever catch up."

Alicia, 56, of Asheboro, North Carolina, who is black, opposes both reparations and a government apology, saying white people today "can't be liable for what their ancestors did." She also questions how a fair amount could be determined.

https://apnews.com/76de76e9870b45d38390cc40e25e8f03

It is comments like these that are the current reality and that is many of are stuck in a place that hinders the brown skinned race. The comments above are the reasons why we must RE-EDUCATE ourselves. Ignorance is no excuse to remain the same. It is everyone's obligation to better our nation.

The mis-education or the improper knowledge is why we as a society has gotten no further. We continue to do what we are instructed to do by systems put in place by the dominate white skinned race. It is each individuals responsibility to improve today because the mentality of future generations is at stake.

We all tend to forget the atrocities that are responsible for the division of mankind even unto this time. Inconspicuous race relations that continue to cripple our nation. Here is a recap of why we must stop the debates and RE-EDUCATE:

Mis – Education	-Vs-	Re – Education
Stagnates a nation, it keeps us stuck in a place of ignorance that perpetuates hate.		Restructures our minds and teaches us to have compassion for one another.

Ignorance is "lack of knowledge" and this is why we must RE-EDUCATE ourselves! The intent of this chapter is not to offend but to direct attention to the mess we are still in because of our own lack of knowledge. I contend that we no longer can sit on the side lines and turn a blind eye. We've all got work to do in order to move the brown skinned race to a better financial place. Proverbs 29:18 "where there is no vision the people perish". People today are literally perishing because they have no vision or hope that their situation will ever change. In their minds they will never come out or get out of the perpetual poverty they were born into. They can see for themselves the disparity of this nation that literally excludes them.

We the people have been suckered by the majority, hook, line and sinker for buying into this so called "Equal

Opportunity Society", again, the Re-education is there is no equal when you have a people that start out behind due to no fault of their own. So many have been duped into believing there is equal chance. The epiphany to me and I hope for you is the successes of a few of us only moves the economic needle for a few us and does nothing to move the needle for the masses of us born into poverty. It will take all of us brown skinned, white skinned, red skinned whatever color your skin to advance the disparity amongst the people.

A side note..

Brown skinned people, we simply cannot remain in IGNORANCE (lack of knowledge). Our IGNORANCE as a people has us engaged and truly focused on the wrong escapades like "Reality TV". The reality is "we started at the bottom and we are still at the bottom", 157 years after Emancipation Proclamation of 1863 set us free, yet disheartening because in reality 400 years counting slavery. We must move from helpless to help fix this mess that continues to hinder the success of brown skinned people. No more excuses for staying the same. We are not a helpless people and we must come together collectively to do and take whatever actions necessary to Re-educate ourselves and help future generations avoid becoming enslaved on the plantation due to the payment of minimum wage.

White skinned people, IGNORANCE (lack of knowledge) is no excuse to stay the same and not engage in the change that needs to take place. You too are responsible for this song "we started at the bottom and we are still here". You are also obligated to help future generations and propel the economic place of a race who because of your dominant control has literally been at the bottom economic pay scale for 400 years and counting. You too must Re-Educate yourselves and dismantle the chains that hinder the brown skinned race.

All people, Ask yourself and seek to find the answers why 157 years of freedom yet more daunting 400 years since slavery a race that started at the bottom is still at the bottom of a country that is so prosperous. Why isn't there prosperity for all? Being bothered by the disparity, out of curiosity I wanted to know the numbers of our current population which confirmed the thoughts I have had along, which are the "Systems of Stagnation" are controlled by the dominant population.

US Census

US 2019 Population – Approximately 329 million
White Majority Race – Approximately 71% of the US Population

Brown/Hispanic Race – Approximately 12% of the US Population

Asian Race & Other – Approximately   5% of the US Population

The majority race is the white skinned race and they own and control just about everything in the US economy.

I conclude IGNORANCE is not bliss it is IGNORANCE and it behooves us ALL to Re-Educate, Re-Activate and Re-Engage because it is ALL of OUR responsibility to make this world a better place, " Lack of knowledge" in

other words IGNORANCE is no excuse! We all have an
obligation to dismantle PLANTATION NATION!

"ENDING POVERTY IS NOT AN ACT OF CHARITY"
It is an act of Justice

Nelson Mandela

Started from the Bottom and we are still "HERE"

We started from the bottom and we are still HERE, similar lyrics to the popular rap song to which my mature ears would bop to each and every time I would hear it being played on the radio. I really like this song! The irony is unlike the positive vibes of the rap song the lyrics of which I write is a negative because I was astonished to learn that brown skinned people are literally sitting in the same place of low economic existence at the bottom of the American economy 157 years after Emancipation Proclamation (the official declaration ordered by Abraham Lincoln in 1863 to FREE the slaves) . Yes, "we started at the bottom and we are still HERE." I know this is hard to believe I too had doubt and unbelief. And had it not been for my own personal experience which is now the lyrics of this book I too would have never known that we are literally sitting in the same place economically which is at the bottom of the economy. Specifically what this means is that out of all the ethnic groups in America brown skinned people are the poorest of them all! Again, I too found it hard to conceive that it has been 400 years since slavery and we have been FREE for 157 years and counting yet we are still at the bottom. As life would have it and I journeyed along and followed my Divine intuition to write this song. I had to see it to believe it and that is time and time again no matter what data I found brown skinned people are at the bottom of the pay scale. This information gave me energized motivation, I had to finish this book. I started to learn being paid a minimum wage was not solely about me but the "Virtual Plantation" that exists today and an even bigger issue is that brown skinned people have a 157 year history of being in last place on the economic scale. Me seeing this number 157 YEARS and hearing it (repeating it to myself....157 YEARS in the rear) bothered me tremendously. I started to question how can this be when I've seen so many brown skinned successful people on TV? Then it occurred to me that I and so many others have been hoodwinked and bamboozled to believe whatever they put on the TV and we tend to believe what we see.

I can hear many of you successful brown skinned brothers and sisters saying "what on earth is she talking about we are doing better as a people, we are FREE to be and pursue whatever endeavors". Yes, I agree, there is no denying that as brown skinned people we have made tremendous strides.... let me paraphrase some of us have made tremendous strides to the point where it looks like we are climbing up the economic ladder.

But the reality is we have few successes in comparison to the masses that start out behind because they are born into generational poverty and then left to fend for themselves in this white skinned dominated society. When we see those few brown skinned on TV living large we are tricked into believing we have made tremendous gains and are no longer enslaved. I too once believed in this so called "Equal

Opportunity" for White Society" along with its various slogans and mantra's to work hard and pursue your dreams. For sure I am in total agreement with the ethics of hard work and there is for sure opportunity in America land of the free, my point is there is no "Equal Opportunity" assisting the brown skinned! Those born into generational poverty tend to remain in generational poverty because they know no other way. My embedded mantra in my mind "mama and daddy cannot teach you what they themselves do not know". In many instances they do not know how to maneuver around the systems in place that keep them stuck in poverty.

Generational Poverty tends to be perpetual, yes tends to be, a few of us will escape its stronghold but masses will remain because they know no other way. Personally speaking if it had not been for all the positive influencers in my life, the teachers, mentors, good white people who encouraged me today I might not have escaped the generational poverty that I was born into. How was my mama with a 9th grade education going to teach me about what she herself did not know!

Oh but GOD if we would only trust and believe that he always has a higher purpose for us and some traumatic things happen for a reason and many times for our good, Romans 8:28. Trust me it was traumatic to go from an $80,000 a year salary to $16 hourly, my 1st thoughts LORD HOW AM I GOING TO MAKE IT? Then my thoughts went to GOD AND HIS PROMISES OF HIGHER PURPOSE, I had to experience it, to get it!

Yes, I REPEAT, I had to experience it to get it! It that is "being paid a minimum wage that virtually enslaves".

GODS HIGHER PURPOSE for me. The seed for this book was planted within me years ago when my eyes could not believe what they would see when they 1st saw the word "plantation", plastered as the name of various housing communities in the southern state of Georgia. I had no clue why I was so bothered by this word and the rest of the world was just humming along as usual as if the casual use of the word means nothing. Quite frankly I was truly then and still quite perplexed why anyone would think this is a good name in which to name anything such as a landmark given its history and what the word means. I'm thinking maybe I have forgotten the meaning of the word so to online resources I go to refresh my memory. I said to myself "maybe I'm just tripp'en, overacting as usual". To my SURPRISE no wonder this word is casually being used because even the dictionary leaves out some truth and defines this word in a soft tone. Are you ready for this... Dictionary.com definition of "Plantation" - 1. a usually large farm or estate, especially in a tropical or semitropical country, on which cotton, tobacco, coffee, sugar cane, or the like is cultivated, usually be resident laborers. Resident Laborers, America has got to get it together and tell the truth to the people! The Plantation was where all the hard brutal work of the bondservant took place so that the white skinned man on his large farm or estate could harvest his cotton, tobacco, coffee, sugar can and the like by SLAVES, his physical owned property to make money. I conclude no I'm not just tripp'en there is an omission of truth, the word is not defined as the truth of what it really means.

I hope that this definition does for you what it does for me which is to propel me into action for the brown skinned people born into perpetual poverty. If I had not been paid a minimum wage, today I might still wrongfully gage the mantra's put out is this society spewing words of "Equality".

It is experience that teaches us best. It is the experience that motivated me to write this book about being paid a low wage. This experience allowed me insight into a world that I too was far removed and that is brown skinned are at the bottom of the pay scale and white skinned are at the top. When you are at the top, which I was, we tend to forget about those at the bottom. I now know by design and not just for security purposes IT (Information Technology) departments and other upward professional positions are separate so they do not intersect and interact with those who are paid a lower wage. IT departments usually exist within their own buildings or floors. Those brown skinned in entry level positions, unless they know someone many times aren't even aware of the professional positions that they should aspire too because if they cannot see or talk to them they cannot aspire to be them. Ironically those who start at entry level in many cases are the true experts because they must learn every detail of what their job entails from beginning to end. Once a certain level of knowledge and experience are obtained the industry refers to this group as "SME's" (Subject Matter Experts) in other words "the employees with the experience and the most knowledge" because they perform the same task day after day. The SME's keep the corporations daily operations up and running. Having worked in both worlds.... I must confess because those of us in "IT" "we get paid a higher wage" for our so called knowledge, but the irony is in many instances we consult with the Subject Matter Experts and cannot complete our jobs without the knowledge of SME's "who are paid a lower wage". The paradox continues, the systems in place reward the white skinned race rather or not they have the knowledge to complete their jobs. They simply continue to take from the brown skinned race they dominate.

A moment of regression,

Prior to writing this book I struggled to articulate. I didn't know why I was so bothered and why I would look around and see (in my opinion) to me we are actually a people going backwards... this would be a constant thought in my head for the most part. Thoughts I would not dare say out loud and mostly because I could not put into audible words how with the education opportunities and with ALL the advancements of technology and the good that it can do, that in many instances when I would see us on social media and TV to me often times we look like a people regressing instead of progressing. I'm such a series person at times and for this reason I'm cautious to what I voice out loud. I do not find humor in what I see in most cases on social media and TV and the focus is on "twerking" and / or disrespecting each other. All I know is it has been difficult for me, I really try to hold my tongue to keep the peace.

It is through writing this book that I am just now able to express the various emotions and I can no longer sit by and watch brown skinned people die if not physically, mentally. I started to realize this book is more than about little bitty old me! I'm at a point where I can no longer keep the peace and I have to do what God has put in me and that is to be the leader he has created me to be and wake up a generation that has literally been asleep. My intuition was talking to me all along and leading me to this destination where I could finally put it down on paper. Those things that instinctively bothered me which is the stagnation of a brown skinned people who have progressed yet regressed at the same time because of successes of a few we continue to get duped. Regress yes this is what it is for me especially when I see what I see on Social Media and on national TV which is disrespect to the 10th degree. I think it is the one thing the white skinned has discovered leave them be and they will kill each other. They just step back and leave us alone and allow us to continue to do harm to our own. The disrespect for each other is off the chain but it is also a part of what literally keeps us in chains. The foolishness of today only perpetuates fighting and hate of a people who has turned on each other like no other. No other race tends to display the same hate. They don't kill each other they help one another. From what I can see in the brown skinned communities there is much work to done to remove the strong hold of racial inequality and generational poverty. It keeps masses confused and focused on the wrong things, enslaved mindsets continues this current decade.

Once upon a time we knew we needed each other, we wouldn't dare turn our backs on our brown skinned sisters and brothers. But many of us, myself included have bought into the delusion that we are doing better as a race… because many of us have bought into the white skinned way. We have literally turned on our own race and have left many behind to deal with their own proverbial issues. We expect those born into generational poverty to know their way out of systems designed to keep them behind. The seed planted in my mind, at the time I had no idea why, many years ago me seeing the word "Plantation" would bother me so. I like many of you, got out of the hood and moved on. I instinctively knew hood life was not for me. I too had moved on but today I'm thankful for the revelation of "PLANTATION NATION" if I had not experienced it, I would not have understood it. And it is there are systems in place that stagnant the brown skinned race. We must return to our roots that helped us survive one of the greatest atrocities experienced by mankind and that was to be chained and sold as slaves. We must help each other as we move forward. I am convinced we need a new revolution if we are in fact going to change the chains of today and propel the brown skinned race to its rightful place. This revolution is not about me or you but about the many who are stuck in a place and may not ever escape, we must do those things God has put in us to do. He has assured me of my assignment to motivate 1 million mindsets out of poverty and your assignment could be the same and that is to propel the advancement of the brown skinned race.

This chapter I leave you with what I finally had to accept and that is 400 years since slavery we are still at the bottom of the American economy. I have listed here data you can view for yourself and I hope these numbers have convinced you there is in fact truth to the lyrics of this song …..

"We started from the bottom and we are still HERE!"

Here is a quick visual provided by the United States Census regarding Race and Poverty

A 51 year glance at brown skinned people being at the bottom of the economy

Data from the US Census / https://www.census.gov

Income and Poverty in the United States: 2018-Current Population Reports

September 2019
JESSICA SEMEGA, MELISSA KOLLAR, JOHN CREAMER, AND ABINASH MOHANTY
REPORT NUMBER P60-266

Data from the Peter G Foundation / https://www.pgpf.org

The Peter G. Peterson Foundation is an American foundation established in 2008 by Peter G. Peterson, former US Secretary of Commerce in the Nixon Administration and co-founder of the Blackstone Group, an American financial-services company.

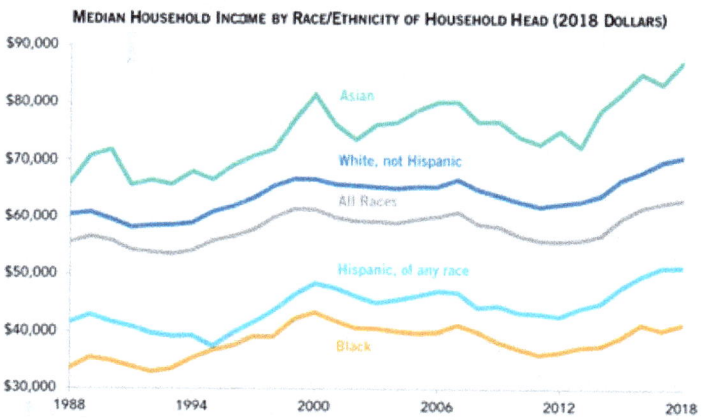

PETER G. PETERSON FOUNDATION — Income varies widely across racial and ethnic groups in the United States

MEDIAN HOUSEHOLD INCOME BY RACE/ETHNICITY OF HOUSEHOLD HEAD (2018 DOLLARS)

SOURCE: United States Census Bureau, Current Population Survey, Annual Social and Economic Supplements.
© 2019 Peter G. Peterson Foundation   PGPF.ORG

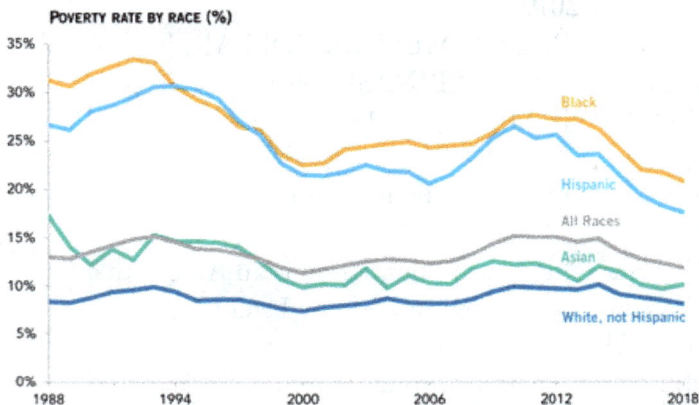

POVERTY RATE BY RACE (%)

SOURCE: United States Census Bureau, Current Population Survey, 2019 Annual Social and Economic Supplement
© 2019 Peter G. Peterson Foundation

Data from Black Demographics / https://blackdemographics.com

Data from Statista / https://www.statista.com
Additionally and concluding words, I really could not find the proper place to mention Asians in this book so I will briefly mention them here.

I find Asians Americans fascinating because they are a small but mighty ethnic group, approximately 6% of the US population, yet they possess more or just as much of the wealth as the white skinned majority who is GIANT in comparison to their size. Admittedly, I currently study them because my next book will be about them! The Asians are doing something right, don't hate on them learn from them. This small but mighty group have been able to escape PLANTATION NATION. They started from the bottom and rose to the top!

Your Gifts, Your Gifts, shall set you FREE!

"When I discover who I am, I'll be free."

Ralph Ellison

Your gifts, your gifts, is what echoes to me as to what will set you free from the strong hold of PLANTATION NATION. I'm thankful that God has given me this revelation to help future generations. I'm so distressed for future generations and that we are steering them right to the plantation which is the "Plantation of Minimum Wage" that will keep them enslaved because of its low wage. I've said many times throughout this book " mommy and daddy cannot teach what they themselves do not know". Momma and daddy only knew to teach survival skills and this is what they instinctively taught us. Life for them was not about flourishing and being fancy free in pursuit of life using ones gifts. It was about being able get a job, any job, that would allow them to eat! And when ones existence is solely focused on surviving they tend to surrender the gifts and dreams that have been implanted in them. So understandably for many, myself included there was never any talk of pursuing dreams or aspirations that would allow you to complete yourself and give your God given gifts to the world and make a living!

Thankfully it is a new day, old things have past and the future is new and brown skinned people must recognize the new time so that they don't continue to lead future generations straight to the plantation.

I wholeheartedly believe in the inspiration given to me that the way off the plantation is the use of our gifts which are our God given natural talents and abilities. This took me many, many years to learn, again, my generation did not grow up in an era where one was encouraged to pursue life endeavors based upon their gifts. As I sat and pondered on many occasions "Lord what is the remedy"? Can people really save themselves and be set free from the plantation? Repeatedly the response echoed to my mind… their gifts, their gifts, shall set them FREE. For ALL have been gifted with innate talents and the great book, the bible says "A man's gifts makes room for him and brings him before the great." Proverbs 18:16 KJV (King James Version), NIV (New International Version) "A gift opens the way and ushers the giver into the presence of the great." The ultimate encouragement from the Divine so much in fact that I must restate "room will be made for YOU and YOU will be ushered in", not only ushered in YOU will be "ushered into the presence of the great". Mama and daddy may be responsible for you being here but they possess no super human powers that allow them to bestow GIFTS! Once more, they can only teach what they know and if they themselves were not taught or encouraged to use their gifts there was no way they were going to be able to encourage you to use yours.

I repeat, GIFTS were not given to just a few of us they were given to ALL of us! We tend to think only those in entertainment are the gifted because…. those we SEE the most we THINK have the most, (the most gifts and talents). Even I have asked Lord why couldn't I have been blessed and gifted like Beyoncé and "J'Lo? When I ask I usually always receive a response in my head which was "song and dance" are not the only gifts needed. The Divine speaking to my mind "it takes all kinds of gifted minds to run this world on mine".

I believe in the Divine and that we are born to use our gifts or they would not be given to us. Our gifts are the sole purpose of us and what the world needs most from us. We weren't given gifts to sit and hide, what good is a gift not given? One more time, if we don't give our gifts we will not be "ushered in"…. natural given gifts are not to be denied or ignored remember it takes all kinds of gifted minds to fulfill the purposes of the Divine.

For sure this world would be a better place if we were taught early on to prepare to serve the world with what we have been given which is our own unique gifts to make this world a better place. Most of human misery indeed is because many are not living who they were born to be. They mis - appropriately serve the world by working in jobs that limit their true inborn capabilities. In other words, the world does not benefit when we don't use our gifts! Most Athletes, Singers, Musicians, Writers don't have to be told they are gifted most naturally know what is in them and most early on get busy learning all they need to learn to be the best at what they are naturally gifted to do. To the beautiful brown skinned whom I like to refer to as "Black Brilliance" I need you to wake up! Stop postponing, ignoring or sleeping on your gifts!

We were all born to make this world a better place and this is not the sole responsibility of the dominate white skinned race. God hasn't gifted us so the we can pursue hate but we 've all been gifted to make Gods world a better place. We all must recognize that it is Gods desire that we all shine.

I had to accept that I'm a gifted writer, which may be open for debate and I'm ok with that. I assure you that I am because I can always think of something to write and say. I was born to write and fight for the people! Here I am most confident, this is my zone it took me some years but I'm so glad that I now know. Putting pen to paper is where I know I am most capable of making this world a better place for the entire human race. I know God has blessed me with a brain that is gifted to think, write and know what to say. Many of you are just like me discovering your gifts later in this life later instead of sooner and I'd like to think that this is because our unique gifts are what is needed in the world now! God knew what and when we were to be when he allowed our parents to create you and me. My gifts for sure where in me all along its just I didn't know because no one ever encouraged me to seek and use those gifts unique to me. For example, for years I have this fascination with studying various businesses across this nation an interest I feel unique to me. I have been gathering information all along that I had no idea would be useful in this book of song that would encourage others to seek to be specifically what God created them to be.

Work your job for sure because you must live and eat, but work your God given talents to live purposefully.

Your gifts, your gifts, will set you FREE and allow you to live purposefully and not remain on the plantation.

One more time, it takes all kinds in order for this world to Divinely shine and if you are of my generation I encourage you today it's not too late to discover your gifts and put them into play.

Parents I have a specific plea to you because your children's futures are at stake... don't allow your struggles, your lack of confidence, your lack of dreaming become their cross to bear. Don't allow your children to remain on the "Plantation of Minimum Wage" the plantation of higher wage, any wage! They were born to serve this world using their gifts and the sooner they know this they will develop into the confident, beautiful, brilliant, flourishing people they are meant to be and they will automatically be paid a wage that will set them FREE. Most importantly they will shine because they will be living out the instruction of the Divine. Parents we must prepare future generations to walk in their greatness, sooner rather than later. Our brown skinned community needs them, they need to be taught early to own their own systems of schools, corporations, and universities so that we can educate and hire our own. We must break this mode of being dependent on others for survival.

The future of our human race depends on the changes we ALL are willing to make. I personally can no longer accept being in the same place economically 157 years later after Emancipation Proclamation yet actuality, 400 years and counting since slavery. This revelation and the experience of being paid a wage that undoubtedly would keep me enslaved propelled me to take action. I hope that I have sparked the activist in you! Together we will dismantle PLANTATION NATION and Your Gifts, Your Gifts shall set YOU FREE!

In Memory of

George Floyd, Breonna Taylor, Ahmaud Arbery, Rayshard Brook, Atatianna Jefferson, Stephon Clark, Botham Jean, Philando Castille, Alton Sterling, Freddie Gray, Eric Garner, Tamir Rice, Michael Brown and so many others who lost their lives so that we live. May you all rest in peace. Your lives were the ultimate sacrifice to inspire the human race to a better place. Your passing has motivated and moved a nation in more ways than you will ever know.

We stand FOR you in unity and will never forget the sacrifice of your lives. YOU are the beacons instrumental in granting us the much needed courage to DISMANTLE PLANTATION NATION. As we move forward YOU ALL ARE THE Guiding LIGHT that leads us to truly make "America Great" and to right the wrongs that have generational strong holds that prevent a people from flourishing in the so called "Land of the Free".

The sacrifice of your lives is the BREATH WE BREATHE. We BREATHE to fight for inequality. We BREATHE to fight for injustice. We BREATHE for a new destiny. We BREATHE a new future. In your names WE BREATHE as we march forward to dismantle the strong hold of racism and its ugliness that entrenches this country.

We will do our part as WE BREATHE to make America a better place as it cannot be "Great Again" as it cannot hold up to such a claim when in fact it has had a people enslaved for generational decades.

So in memory of YOU ALL WE BREATHE

Social Media

For now, I have decided to reside in the sunny state of Florida, I'd love to connect on Social Media.

Inspire your love ones and purchase books via the WEB!

www.dismantlingplantationnation.com

FACEBOOK / FB
MovingForwardDismatlingPlantationNation@
PlantationNationUSA

TWITTER / TWEET
DismantlingPlantationNation
@PlanationNation_USA

INSTA
DismantlingPlantationNation / PlantationNationUSA

EMAIL
Michellewhitby@yahoo.com

TOGETHER we will dismantle
PLANTATION NATION!